Rule the Kingdom
in plastic canvas

Humble plastic canvas takes on a regal status with Nicole Barrett's costume ensembles. Three sizes allow the crowns to fit ages 2 to 10.

King Edward 2

Princess Lily 8

King Henry 16

Plastic Canvas Basics 27

Meet the Designer 28

I0877628

LEISURE ARTS, INC. • Maumelle, Arkansas

King Edward

SUPPLIES

- ☐ medium weight yarn (refer to color key on page 4)
- ☐ 7 mesh plastic canvas – two $13^1/_2$" x $21^1/_2$" sheets
- ☐ $^5/_{16}$" diameter x $18^1/_2$" long wood dowel
- ☐ polyester fiberfill
- ☐ #16 tapestry needle

Crown Sizes:
Small (19" circumference)
Medium (20" circumference)
Large (21" circumference)

Scepter: $3^3/_4$" wide x $21^1/_2$" high

To make the Crown:

1. For the Small and Medium Crowns, follow the chart to cut out and stitch the Crown using 2 strands of yarn and leaving the purple shaded area unworked. Matching the orange triangles, work the stitches in the purple shaded area to join the Crown into a ring.

2. For the Large Crown, follow the charts to cut out and stitch the pieces using 2 strands of yarn and leaving the purple shaded areas unworked. Matching symbols, work the stitches in the purple shaded area to join the Crown pieces into a ring.

3. For the Inner Band, cut a canvas piece:
   Small –126 x 7 threads
   Medium –137 x 7 threads
   Large –144 x 7 threads

4. Bend the band into a circle with the short ends butted together; join the butted edges with lt blue Overcast Stitches.

5. Matching the bottom edge of the Crown with one edge of the Inner Band, place the band inside the Crown (it should be a tight fit); use lt blue to join the bottom edges. ***Note:*** Because the Inner Band is a few threads smaller than the Crown, not all holes will line up exactly. There will be times you will need to stitch through the same hole several times on the Inner Band, but remain consistent going through each Crown hole twice. The Crown top edge is unworked.

To make the Scepter:

1. Follow the chart to cut out and stitch Scepters using 2 strands of yarn for Gobelin Stitches.

2. Place the Scepters wrong sides together; use grey Overcast Stitches to join the Scepters along the rounded top and one side, stopping at the lower point.

3. Place the dowel between the canvas pieces. Fill the rounded top of the Scepter with fiberfill.

4. Continue joining with Overcast Stitches through both pieces until you reach your starting point.

COLOR KEY

- lt blue (35 yards)
- blue (8 yards)
- grey (44 yards)
- black (1 yard)

Chart Note: The chart of the Scepter represents one 26 x 145 thread canvas piece. It is split to make it large enough to be followed easily. The threads in the bracketed sections of the chart are repeated from one section to the next to accommodate the length of the stitches. No stitches are repeated from one section to the next.

Scepter

(26 x 145 threads) (stitch 2)

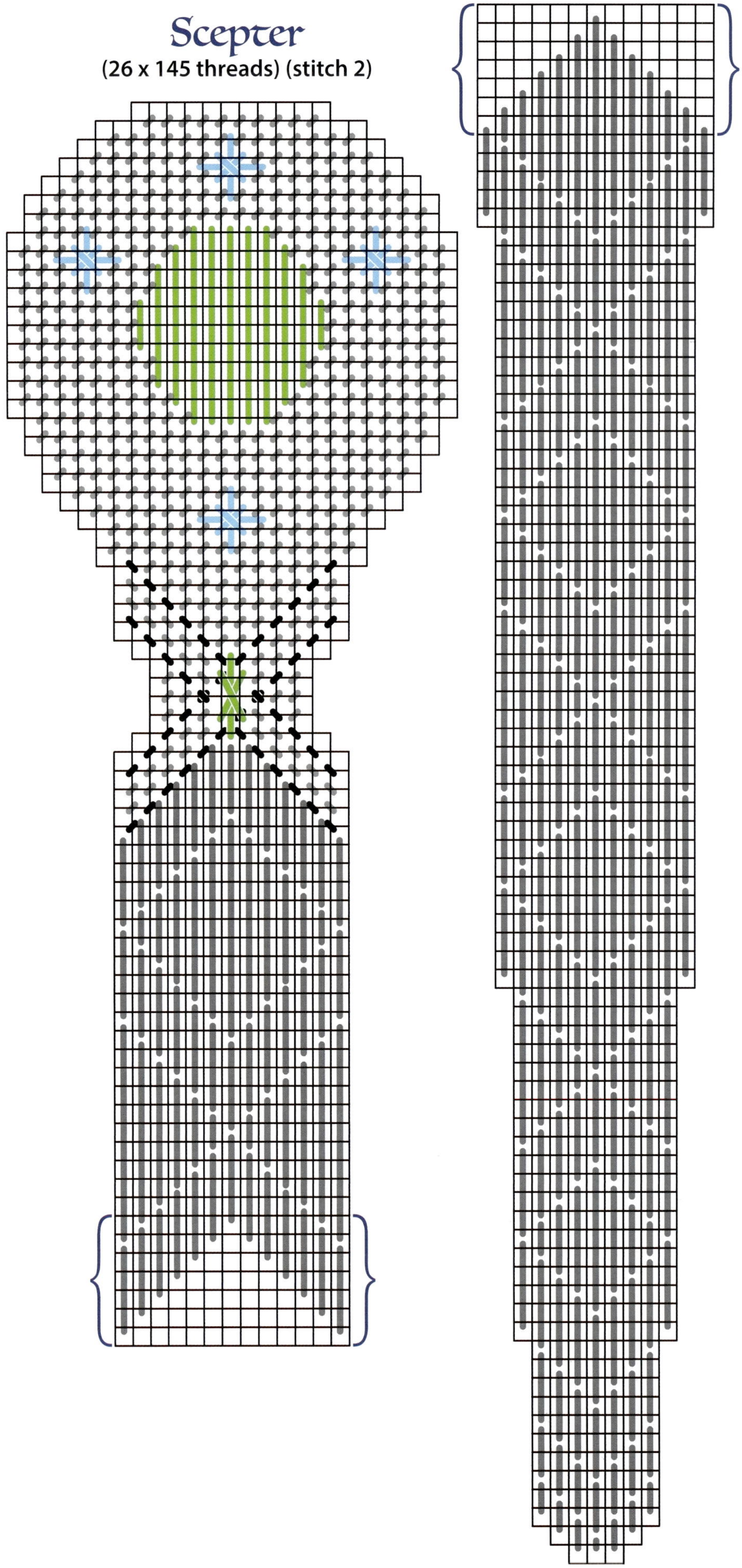

Small Crown

(135 x 25 threads) (stitch 1)

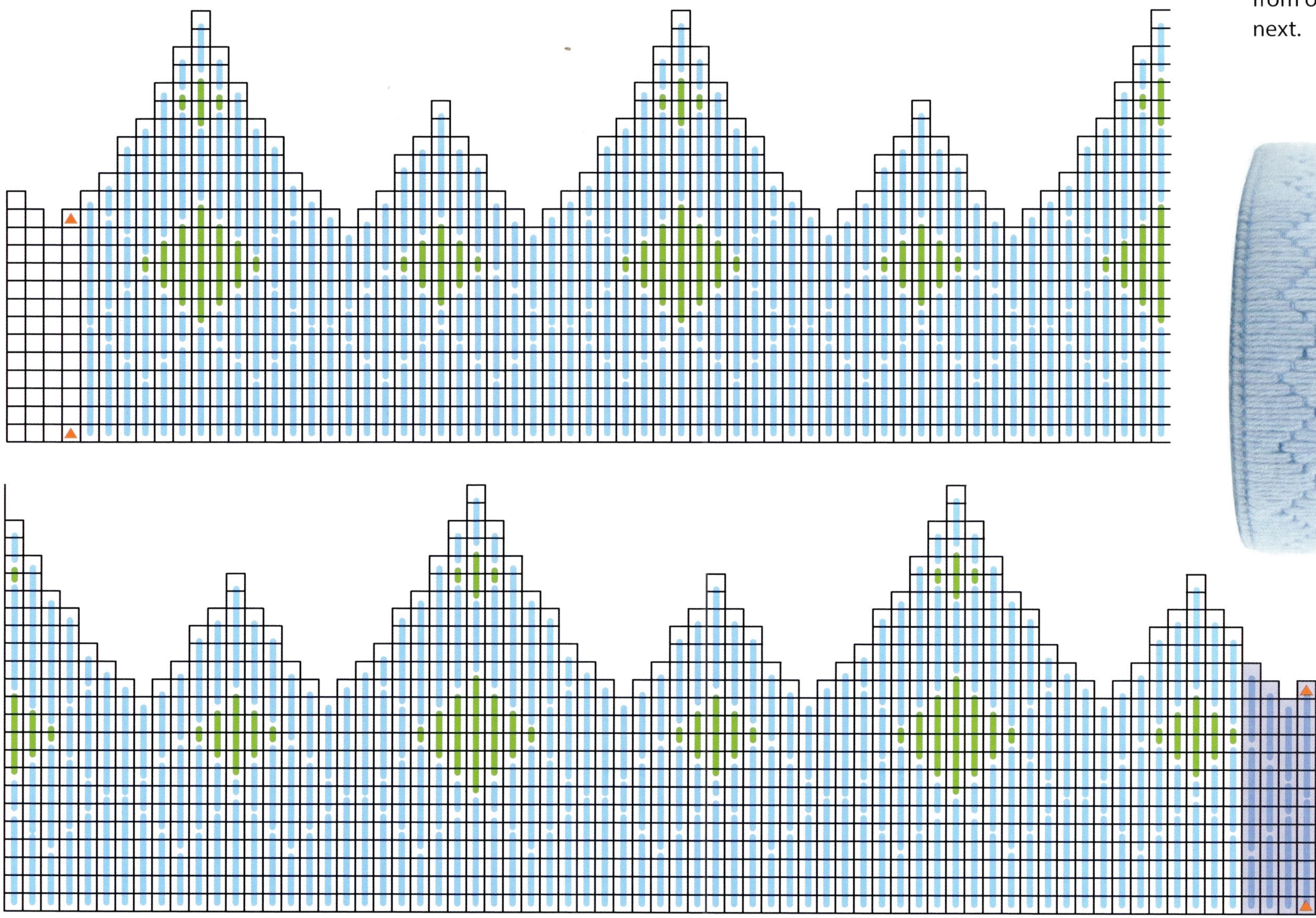

Chart Note: The chart of the Small Crown represents one 135 x 25 thread canvas piece. It is split to make it large enough to be followed easily. No threads or stitches are repeated from one section to the next.

Medium Crown

(144 x 25 threads) (stitch 1)

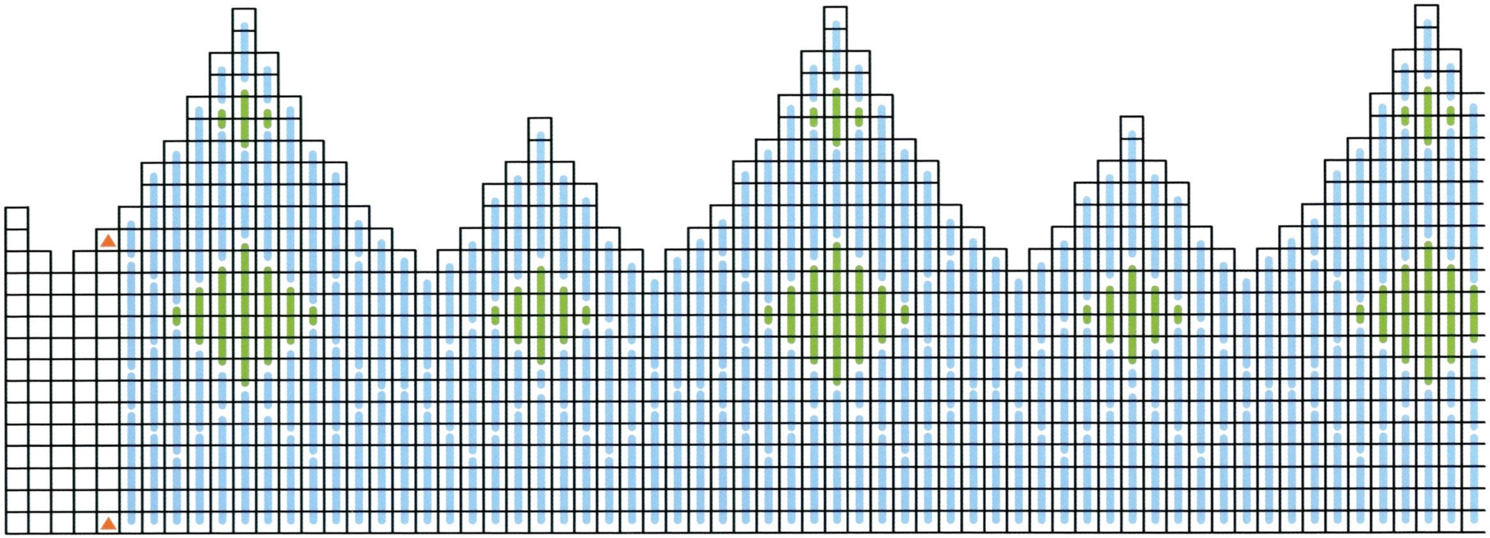

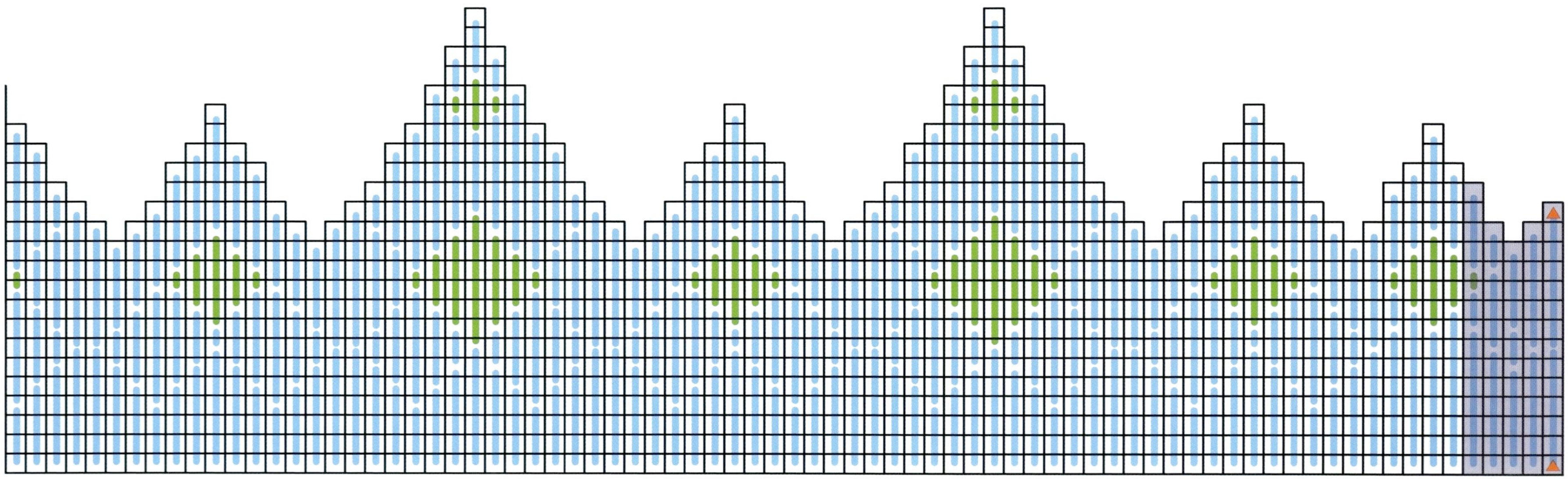

Chart Note: The chart of the Medium Crown represents one 144 x 25 thread canvas piece. It is split to make it large enough to be followed easily. No threads or stitches are repeated from one section to the next.

COLOR KEY

- lt blue
- blue

Chart Note: The chart of the Large Crown represents one 135 x 25 thread canvas piece. It is split to make it large enough to be followed easily. No threads or stitches are repeated from one section to the next.

Large Crown

(135 x 25 threads) (stitch 1)

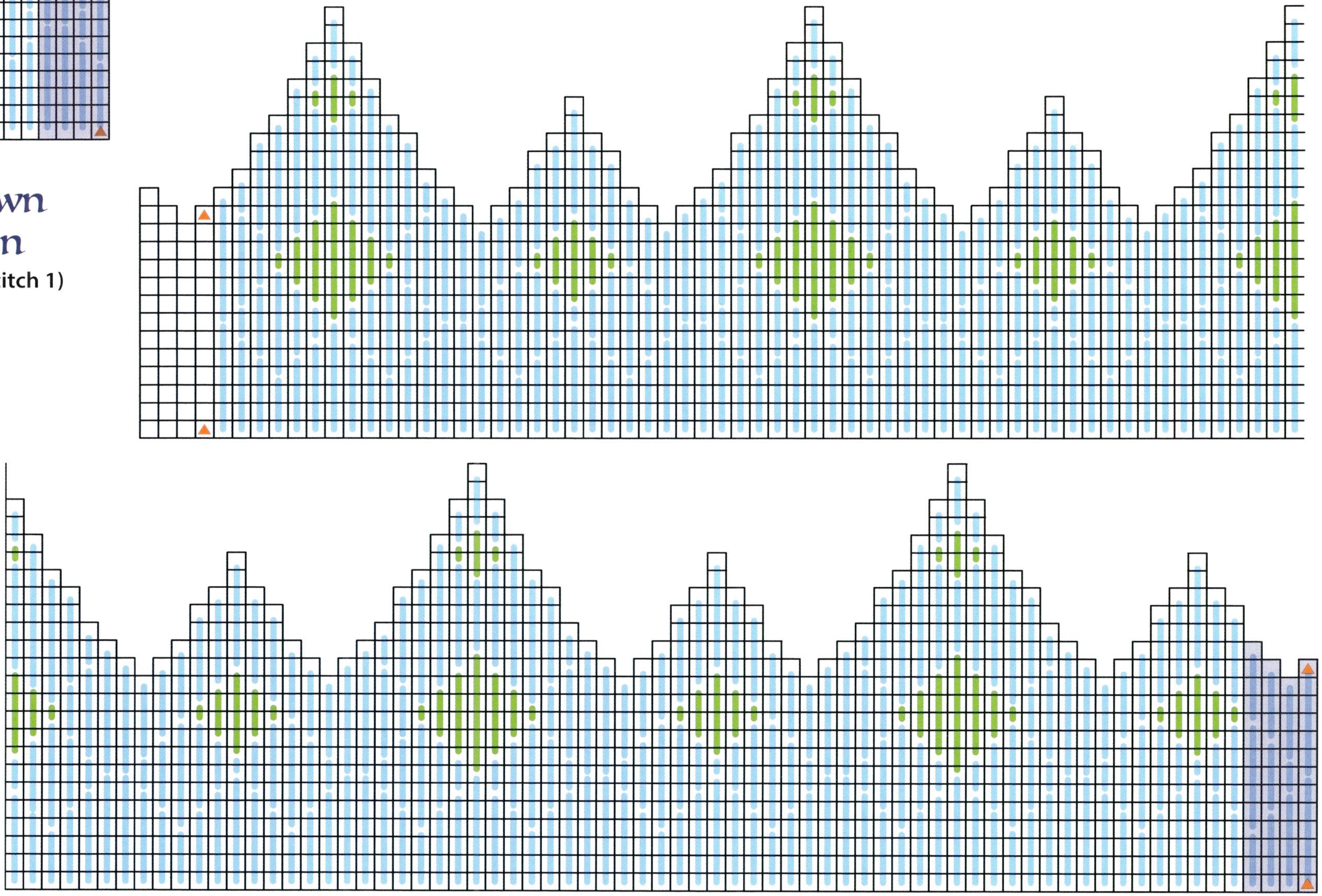

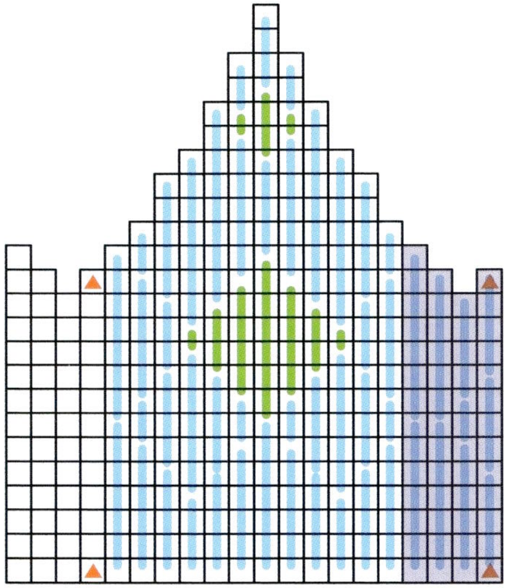

Large Crown Extension

(21 x 25 threads) (stitch 1)

Princess Lily

SUPPLIES

- ☐ medium weight yarn (refer to color keys on pages 11 and 14)
- ☐ 7 mesh plastic canvas – three $13^1/_2$" x $21^1/_2$" sheets
- ☐ two $3^1/_4$" plastic canvas stars
- ☐ $^5/_{16}$" diameter x 16" long wood dowel
- ☐ polyester fiberfill
- ☐ 13mm decorative acrylic jewels
- ☐ 15" x 15" piece of black felt
- ☐ 1 yard of $^3/_8$" wide elastic
- ☐ hot glue gun and glue sticks
- ☐ #16 tapestry needle
- ☐ sewing thread and a hand sewing needle

Crown Sizes:
Small ($19^1/_2$" circumference)
Medium ($20^3/_4$" circumference)
Large ($22^1/_2$" circumference)

Wand: $3^1/_2$" wide x $16^3/_4$" long

Wings: $13^1/_2$" wide x 13" high

Bracelets: $7^7/_8$" circumference each

To make the Crown:

1. For Small Crown, follow the chart to cut out and stitch the Crown, leaving the purple shaded areas unworked. Matching the green triangles, work the stitches in the purple shaded areas to join the Crown into a ring.

2. For Medium or Large Crown, follow the charts to cut out and stitch the Crown pieces, leaving the purple shaded areas unworked. Matching the green triangles, work the stitches in the purple shaded areas to join the Crown into a ring.

3. For the Inner Band, cut a canvas piece:
   Small – 133 x 6 threads
   Medium – 139 x 6 threads
   Large – 146 x 6 threads.

4. Bend the Inner Band into a circle with the short ends butted together; join the butted edges with yellow Overcast Stitches.

5. Matching the bottom edge of the Crown with one edge of the Inner Band, place the band inside the Crown (should be a tight fit); use yellow to join the bottom edges. ***Note:*** Because the Inner Band is a few threads smaller than the Crown itself, not all holes will line up exactly. There will be times you will need to stitch through the same hole several times on the Inner Band, but remain consistent going through each Crown hole twice.

6. Overcast the top edge of the crown with yellow.

7. Glue decorative jewels to the crown as desired.

To make the Wand:

1. Follow the chart to stitch the Stars using 2 strands of yarn.

2. Use yellow Overcast Stitches to join the star pieces along the unworked edges; leave the yarn and needle attached.

3. Carefully place a small amount of glue between the stars; insert about 2" of the dowel through the opening and allow glue to harden.

4. Wrap the attached yarn around the dowel at the base of the star; tuck the yarn end into the star opening and secure with glue.

5. Center and glue a decorative jewel to each side of the star.

Continued on page 13.

Chart Note: The chart of the Crown represents one 140 x 28 thread canvas piece. It is split to make it large enough to be followed easily. No threads or stitches are repeated from one section to the next.

Crown

(140 x 28 threads) (stitch 1)

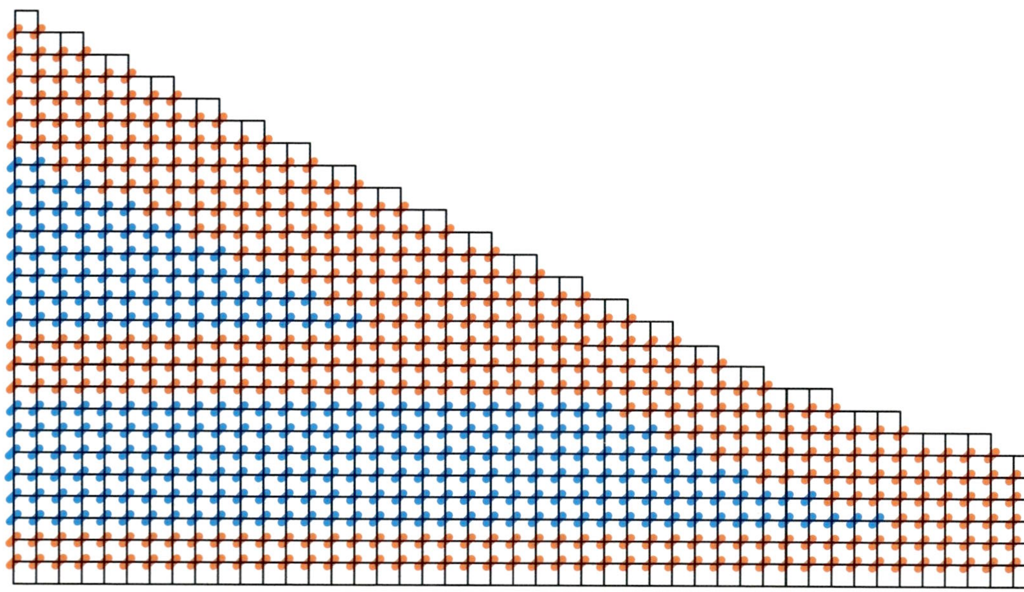

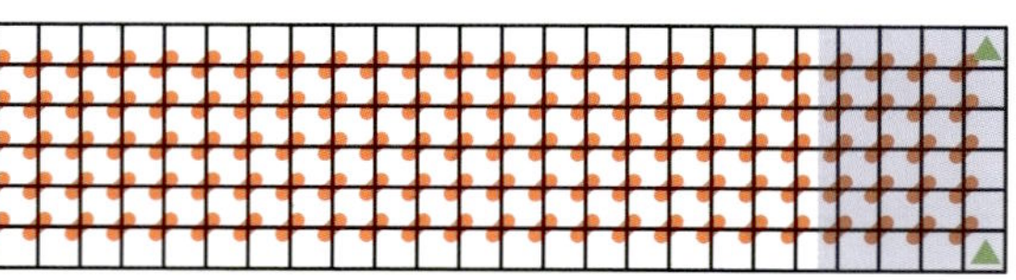

Large Extension

(24 x 7 threads) (stitch 1)

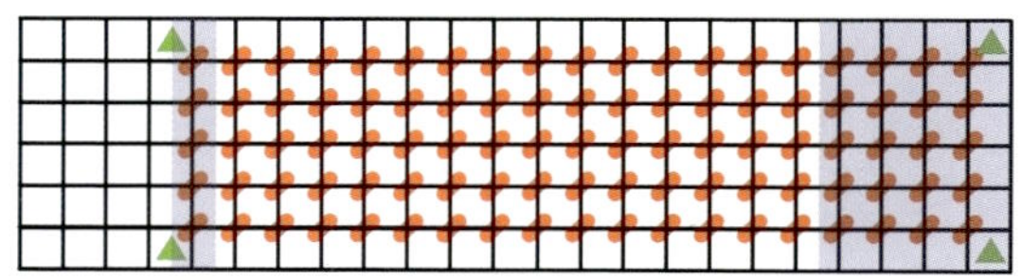

Medium Extension

(18 x 7 threads) (stitch 1)

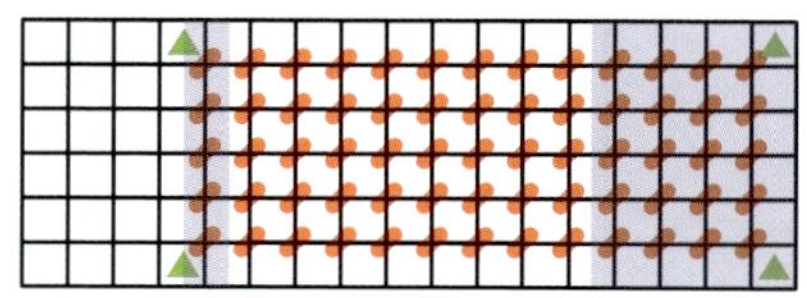

COLOR KEY

- yellow (31 yards)
- vy lt yellow (12 yards)
- bracelet colors: white, vy lt yellow, orange, light pink, blue, magenta (2 yards each)

Star

(stitch 2)

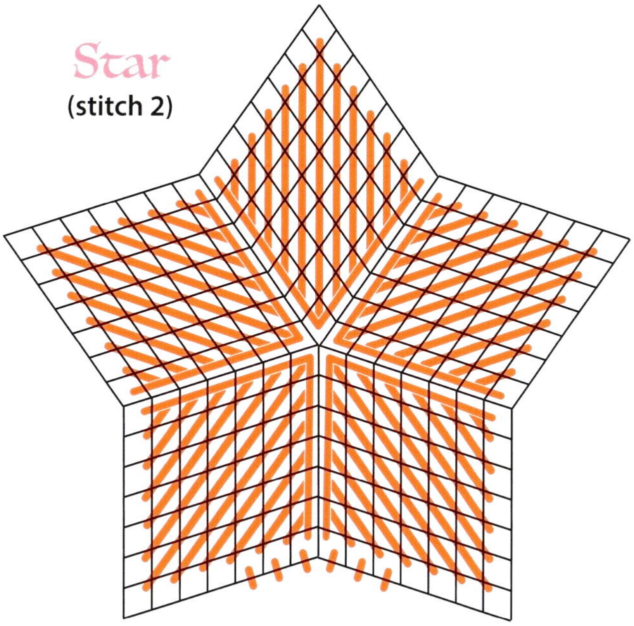

Bracelet

(55 x 3 threads)

Wing Back

(90 x 87 threads) (cut 1)

Chart Note: The chart of the Wing Back represents one 90 x 87 thread canvas piece. It is split to make it large enough to be followed easily. No threads are repeated from one section to the next.

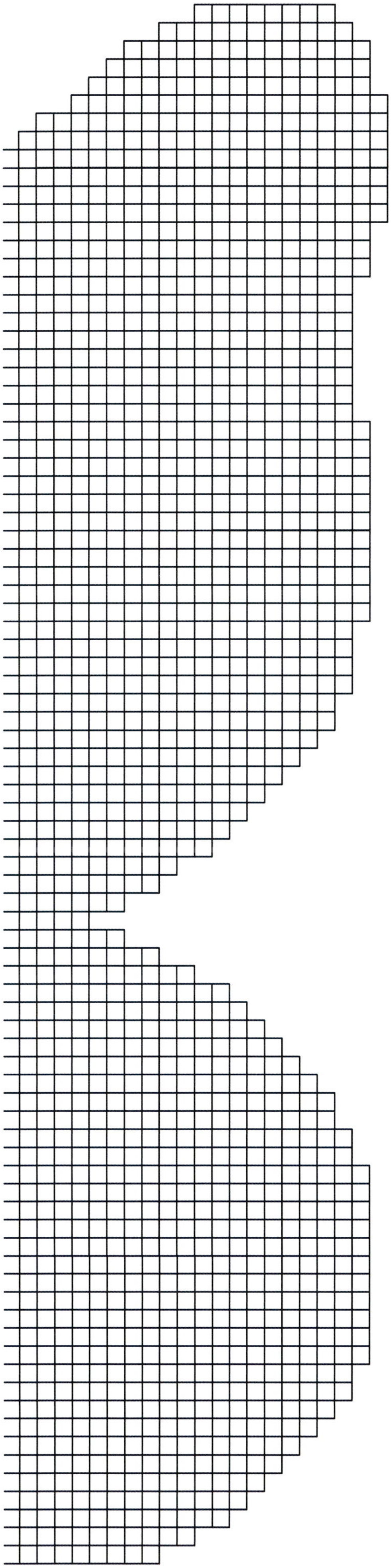

To make the Wings:

1. Follow the charts to cut out a Wing Front and a Wing Back; stitch the Wing Front using 2 strands of yarn for all stitches except black Tent Stitches and vy lt yellow Cross Stitches.

2. On the Wing Back, cut and remove the threads as indicated on the chart.

3. Cut the elastic into two 18" lengths. Thread the ends of one elastic length through the top and bottom openings on the left side of the Wing Back; overlap ends by 1/2" and hand sew to secure. Repeat with the remaining elastic length on the right side.

4. Making sure the elastic overlaps are sandwiched between the layers, place the Wing pieces back to back. Work stitches in the blue shaded area of Wing Front to join the pieces. Stitching through both layers, use black Overcast Stitches to join the pieces along the unworked edges.

5. To make the felt lining pattern, draw around the Wings on paper; cut out the pattern. Use the pattern to cut a felt lining. Glue the lining to Wing Back, clipping the felt as necessary to go around the elastic pieces.

To make each Bracelet:

1. Follow the chart to cut out and stitch the bracelet, leaving the grey shaded areas unworked.

2. Matching the blue triangles, work the stitches in grey shaded areas to join the bracelet.

3. Use matching color Overcast Stitches to cover the unworked edges.

4. Glue decorative jewels to the bracelet as desired.

Wing Front

(90 x 87 threads) (stitch 1)

COLOR KEY

- vy lt yellow
- lt purple (12 yards)
- dk purple (20 yards)
- pink (12 yards)
- tan (12 yards)
- black (40 yards)

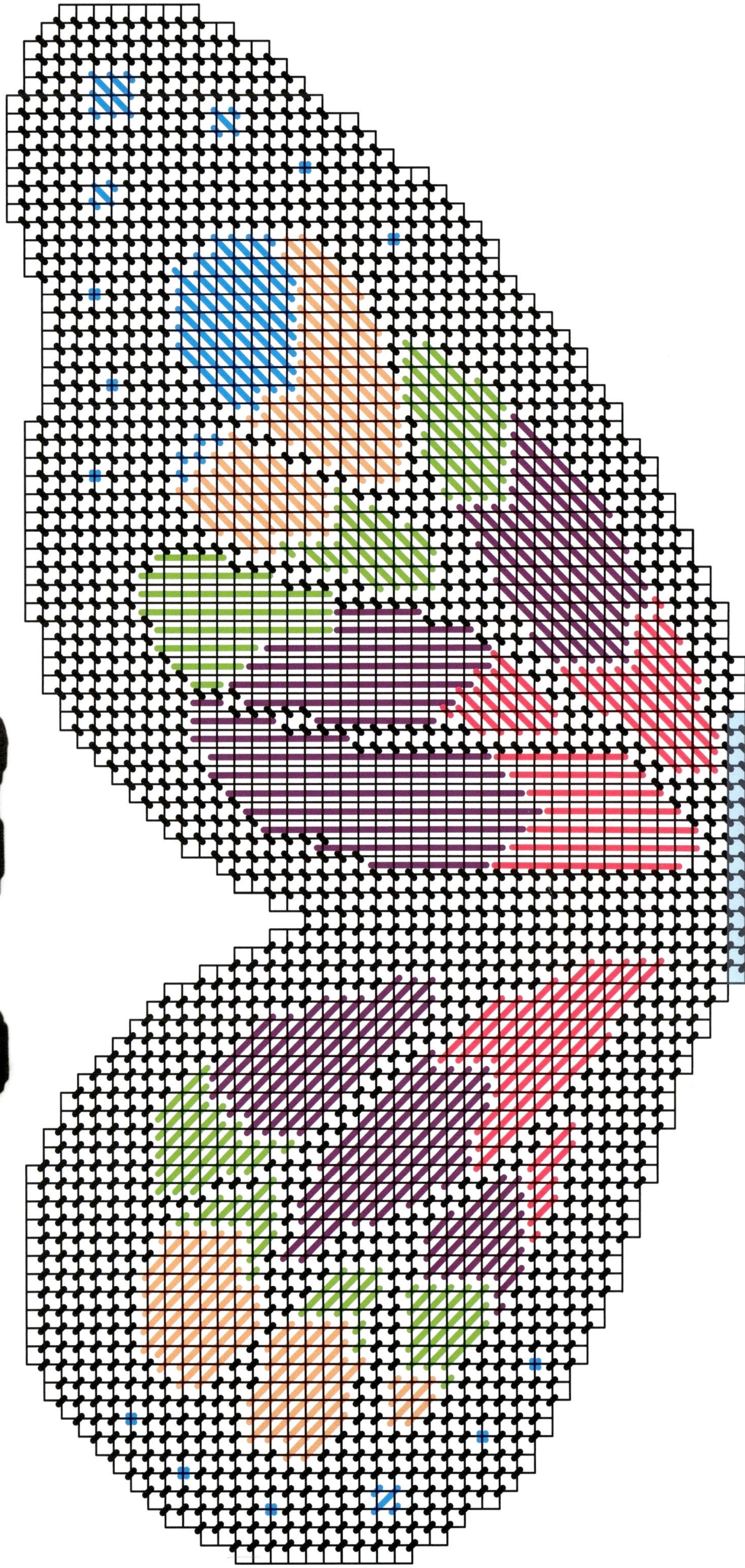

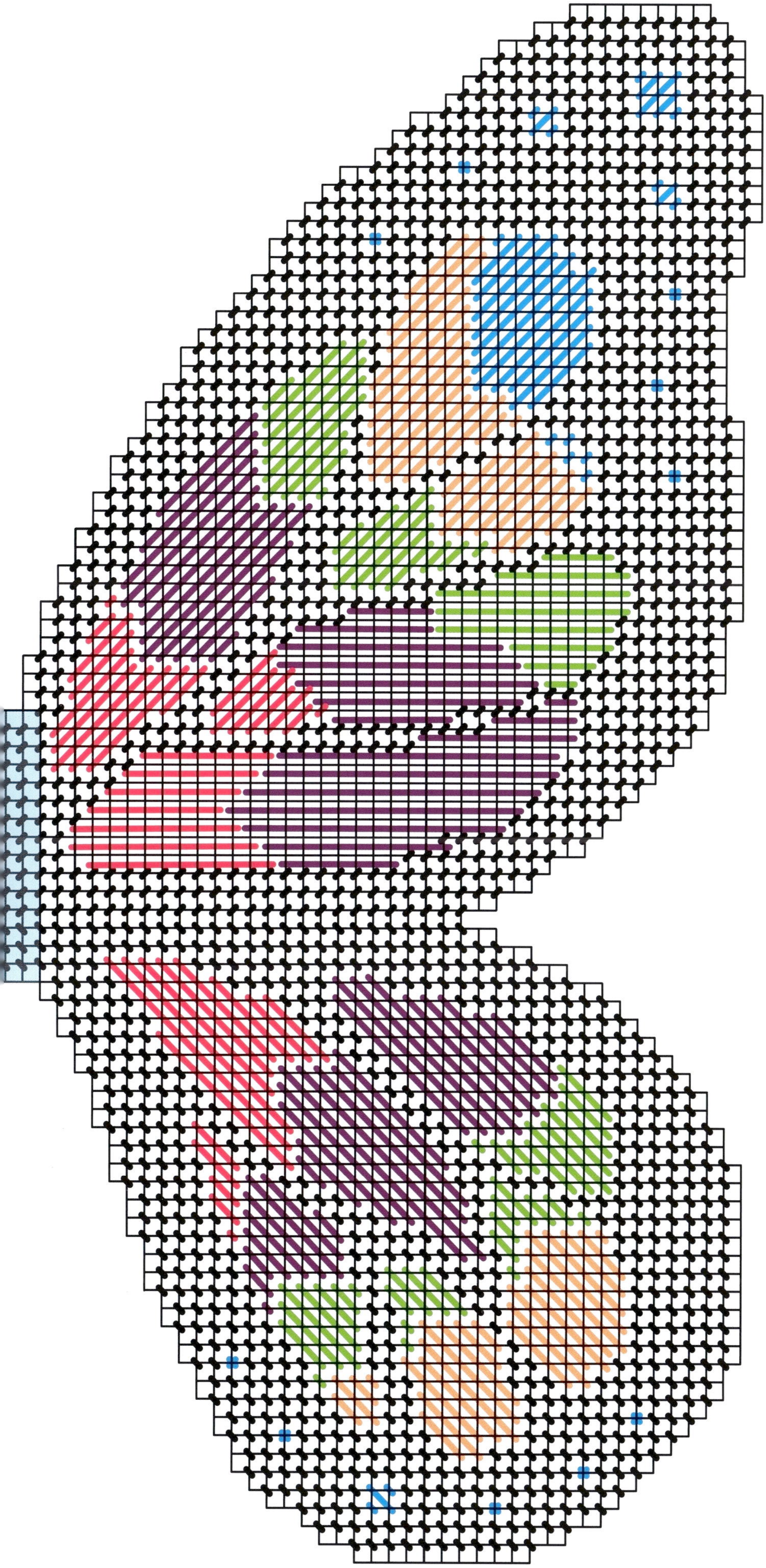

King Henry

SUPPLIES

- ☐ medium weight yarn (refer to color keys on pages 24 and either 18, 20, or 22)
- ☐ 7 mesh plastic canvas - five $13^1/_2$" x $21^1/_2$" sheets
- ☐ $^5/_{16}$" diameter x $20^1/_2$" long wood dowel
- ☐ #16 tapestry needle

Crown Sizes:
Small (20" circumference)
Medium (21" circumference)
Large (22" circumference)

Sword: $7^1/_2$" wide x 22" long

Shield: $10^1/_2$" wide x $13^1/_2$" high

Fig. 1

To make the Crown:

1. For the Small Crown, follow the chart to cut out and stitch the Crown using 2 strands of yarn for the Gobelin Stitches and leaving the grey shaded area unworked. Matching the blue stars, work the stitches in the grey shaded area to join the Crown into a ring.

2. For the Medium or Large Crown, follow the charts to cut out and stitch the Crown pieces using 2 strands of yarn for the Gobelin Stitches and leaving the grey shaded areas unworked. Matching the symbols, work the stitches in the grey shaded areas to join the Crown pieces into a ring.

3. Use red Overcast Stitches to join the angled sides of the red sections of the Crown.

4. Referring to **Fig. 1**, slightly overlap and tack the gold sections together.

5. Follow the chart to stitch a Crown Button; leave a long yarn tail. Place the stitched button on top of the gold joined crown points; place the unstitched button inside the crown, under the joined red area. Pulling firmly to bring the two buttons together, stitch up and down though all the layers 3-4 times; secure with a knot on the inside of the crown.

6. For the Inner Band, cut a canvas piece or pieces:
   Small – **one** 135 x 9 threads
   Medium – **one** 146 x 9 threads
   Large – **two** 76 x 9 threads

7. For the Small or Medium Inner Band, butt the short ends of the band together; join with gold Overcast Stitches to form a ring. For the Large Inner Band, butt the ends together and join the pieces with gold to make one long band before joining into a ring.

8. Matching the bottom edge of the Crown with one edge of the Inner Band, place the band inside the Crown (it should be a tight fit); use gold to join the bottom edges. ***Note:*** Because the Inner Band is a few threads smaller than the Crown, not all holes will line up exactly. There will be times you will need to stitch through the

same hole several times on the Inner Band, but remain consistent going through each Crown hole twice.

To make the Shield:

1. Follow the charts to cut out and stitch the Shield and Shield Handles, using 2 strands of yarn for the stitches on the Shield.
2. Matching green squares, work stitches in the pink shaded areas to join Handles to the unstitched Shield.
3. With wrong sides together and stitching through both layers, use grey Overcast Stitches to join the Shield pieces.

To make the Sword:

1. Follow the chart to cut out and stitch Swords.
2. Place the Swords wrong sides together; use grey Overcast Stitches to join the Swords along the hilt and one side, stopping at the blade tip.
3. Place the dowel between the canvas pieces, inserting one end into the hilt.
4. Continue to work Overcast Stitches through both pieces until you reach your starting point.

Small Crown

(143 x 57 threads) (stitch 1)

Chart Note: The chart of the Small Crown represents one 143 x 57 thread canvas piece. It is split into two sections to make it large enough to be followed easily. The threads in the bracketed areas of the chart are repeated from one section to the next to accommodate the length of the stitches. No stitches are repeated from one section to the next.

COLOR KEY

- gold (90 yards)
- red (50 yards)

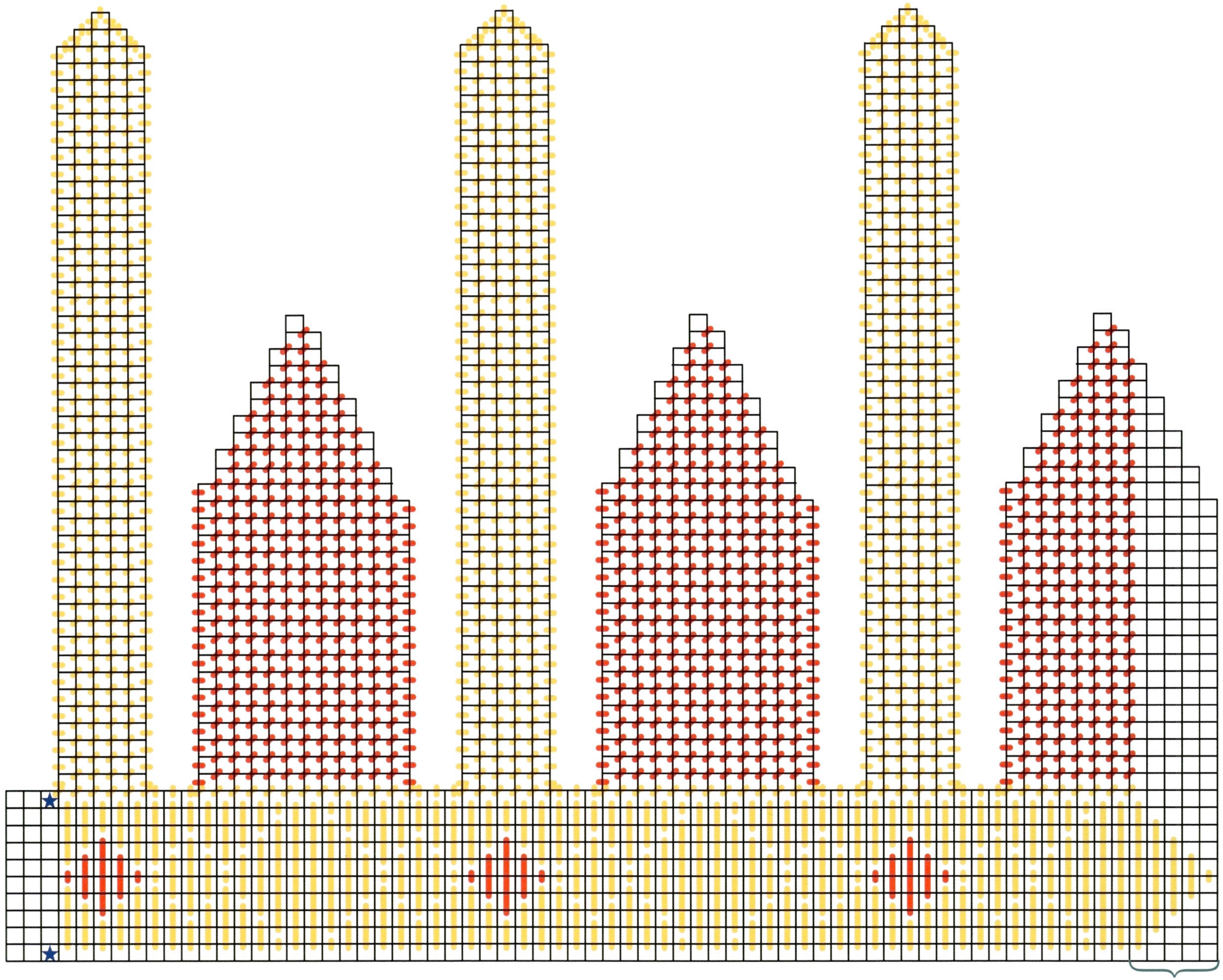

Crown Button

(5 x 5 threads) (cut 2, stitch 1)

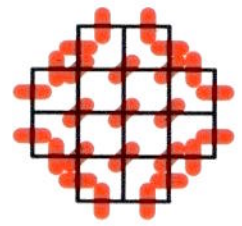

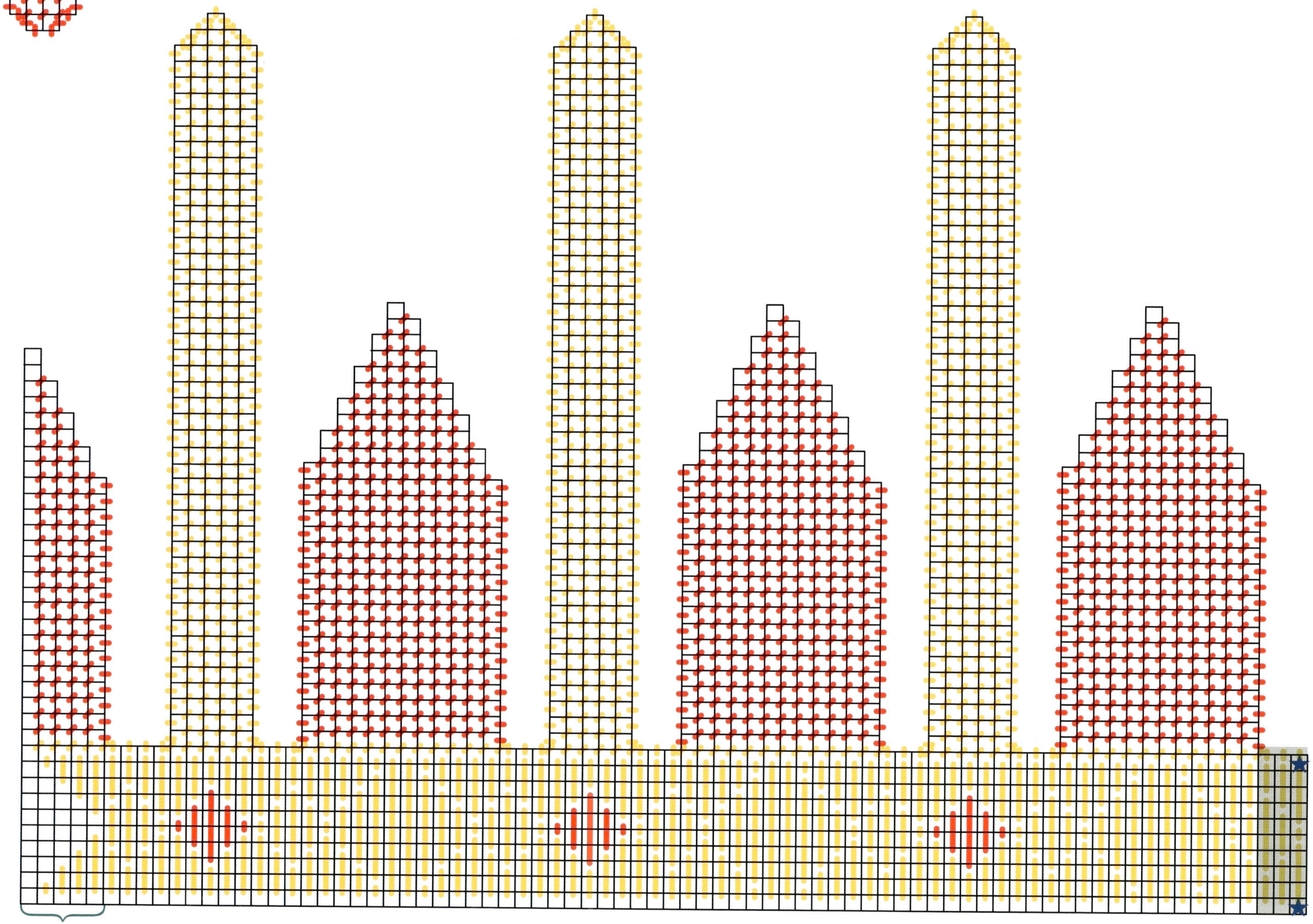

Medium Crown A

(79 x 59 threads) (stitch 1)

COLOR KEY
- gold (95 yards)
- red (52 yards)

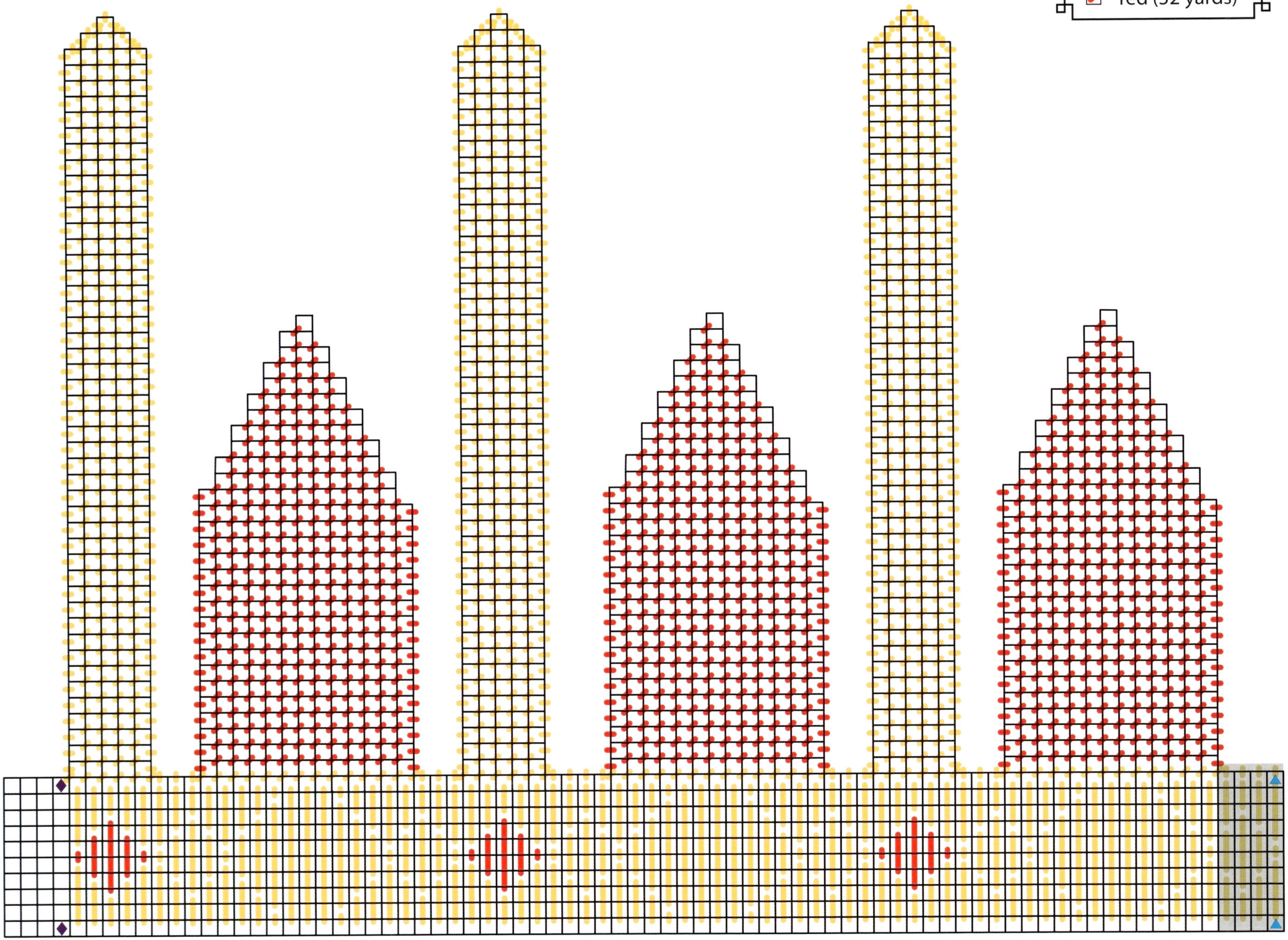

Medium Crown B

(79 x 59 threads) (stitch 1)

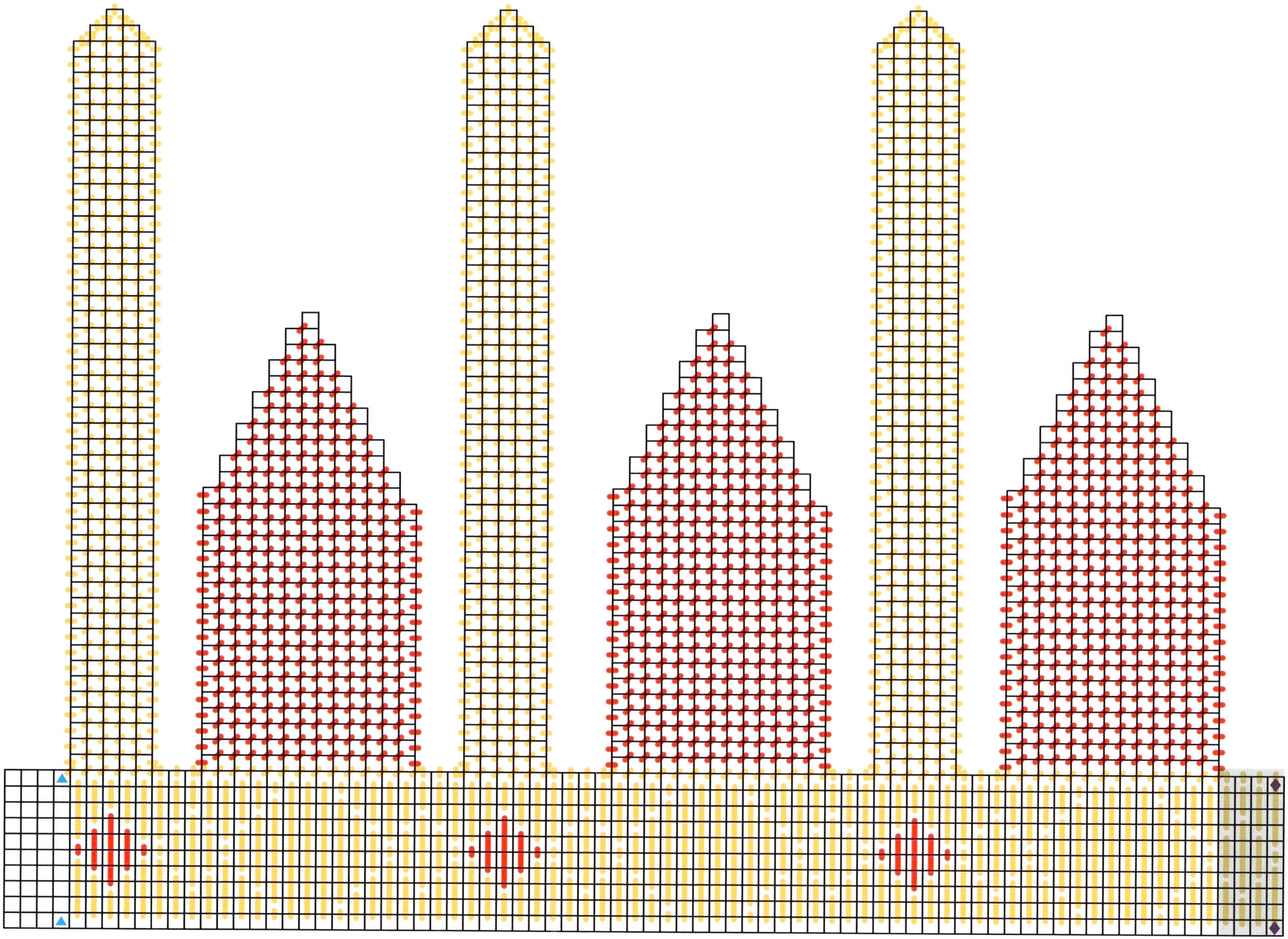

Large Crown A

(82 x 60 threads) (stitch 1)

COLOR KEY

- gold (100 yards)
- red (56 yards)

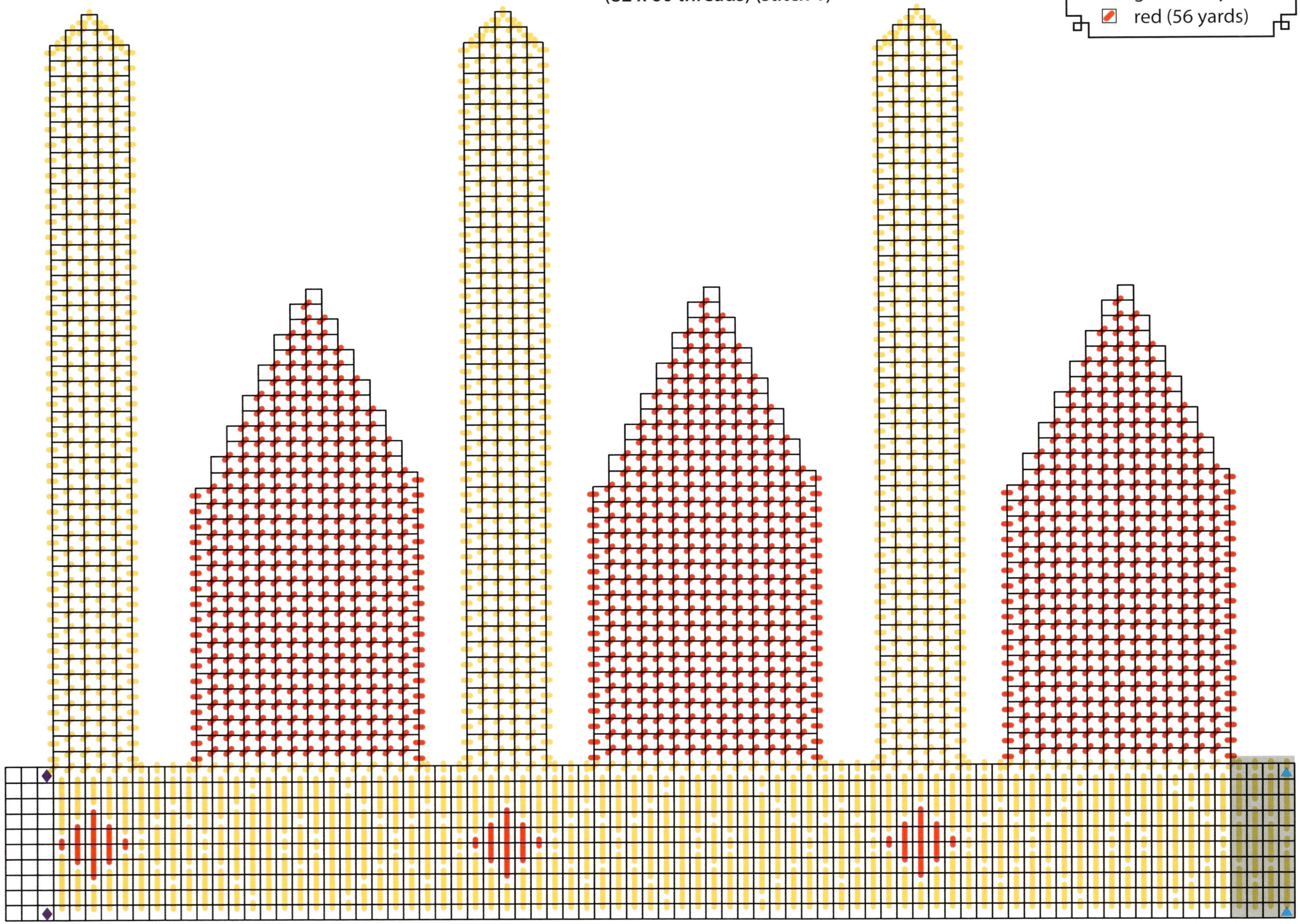

Large Crown B

(82 x 60 threads) (stitch 1)

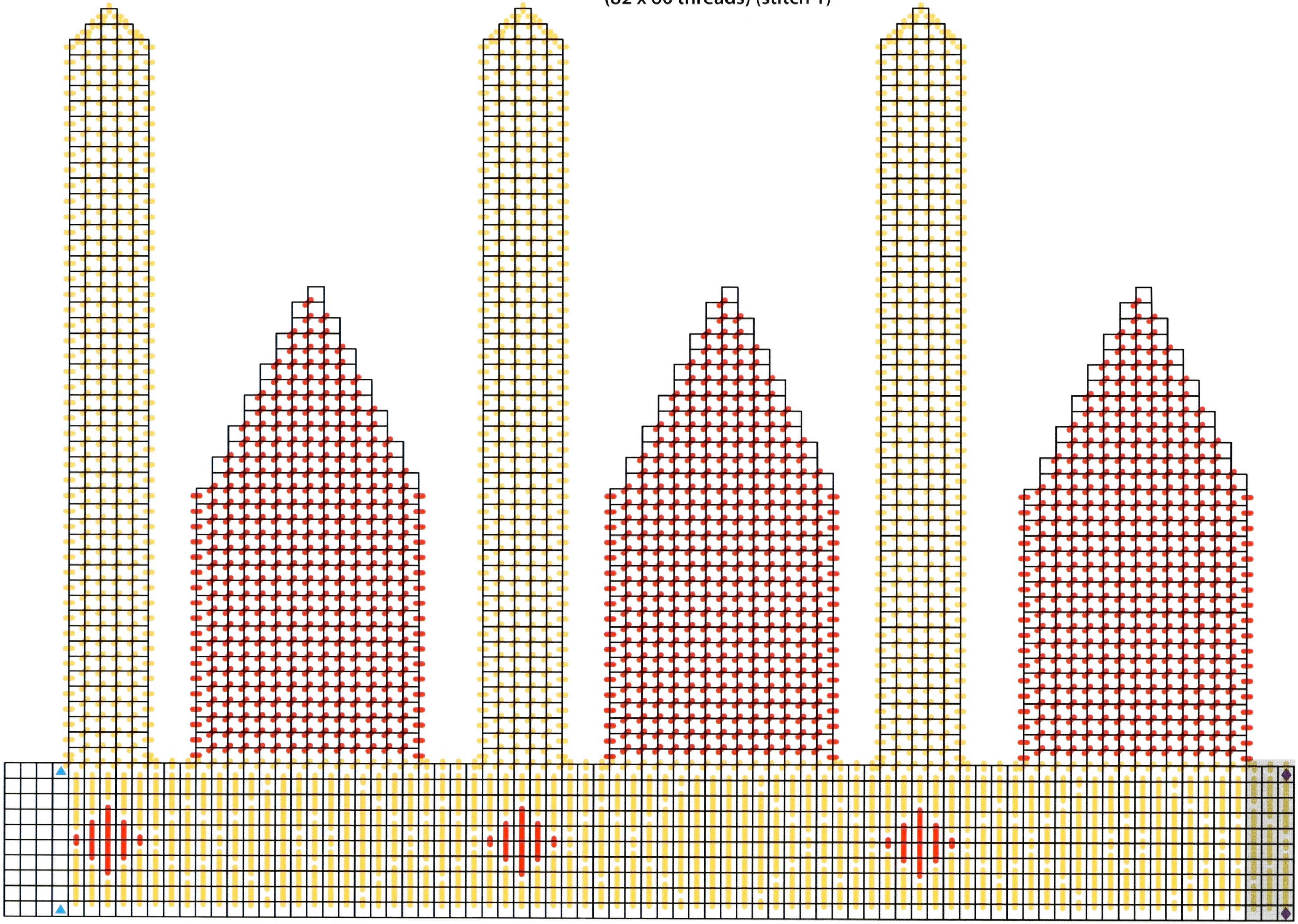

Chart Note: The chart of the Shield Front/Back represents one 71 x 91 thread canvas piece. It is spread across two pages to make it large enough to be followed easily. The threads in the bracketed sections of the chart are repeated from one page to the next to accommodate the length of the stitches. No stitches are repeated from one page to the next.

COLOR KEY

- grey (162 yards)
- gold
- red

Shield Front/Back

(71 x 91 threads) (cut 2, stitch 1)

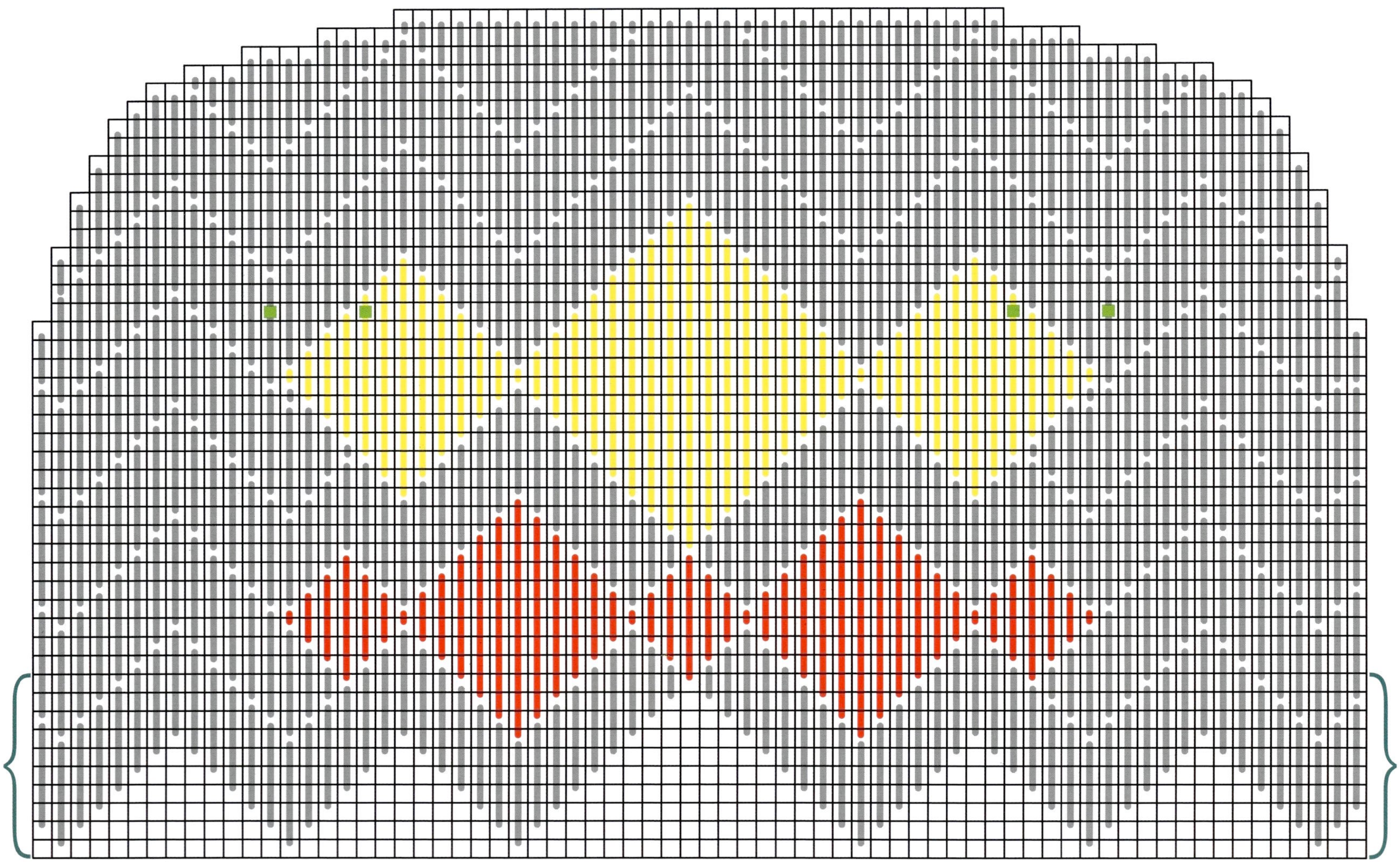

Shield Handle

(7 x 45 threads) (stitch 2)

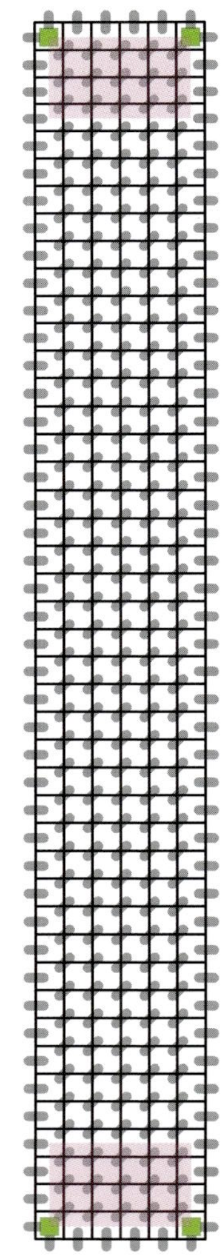

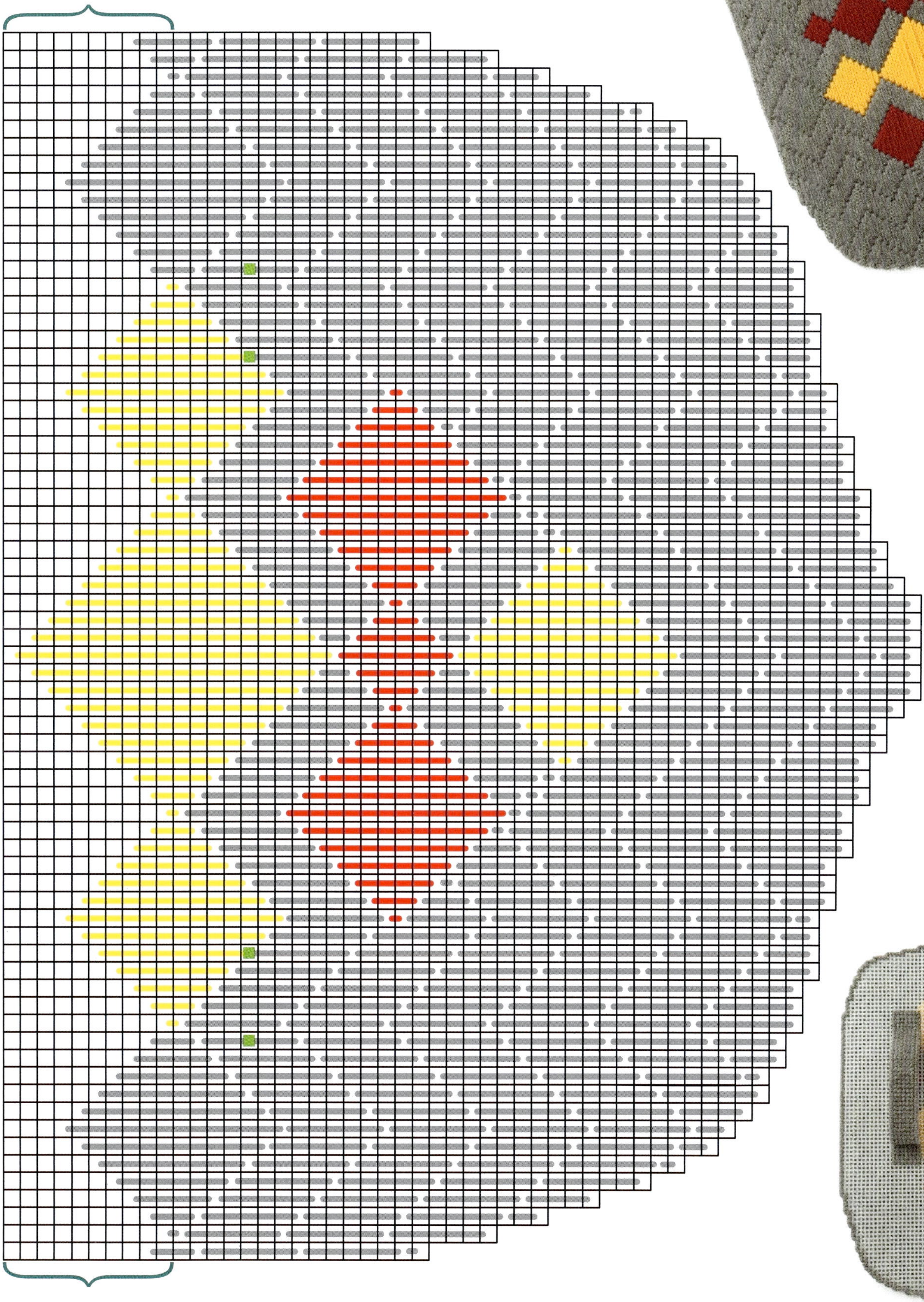

COLOR KEY

- grey
- gold
- red

Chart Note: The chart of the Sword represents one 50 x 147 thread canvas piece. It is broken into two sections to make it large enough to be followed easily. The threads in the bracketed areas of the chart are repeated from one section to the next to accommodate the length of the stitches. No stitches are repeated from one section to the next.

Sword

(50 x 147 threads) (stitch 2)

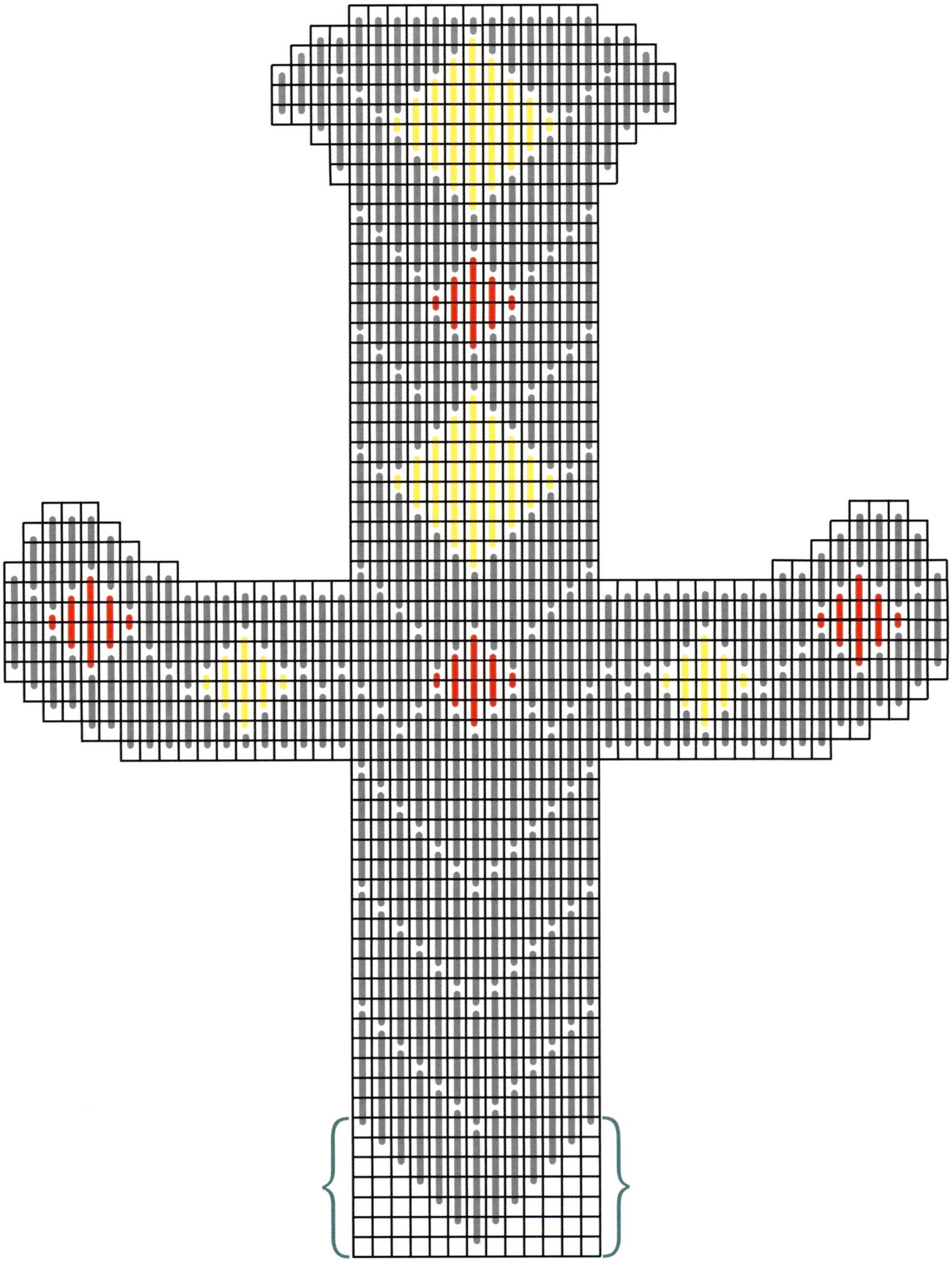

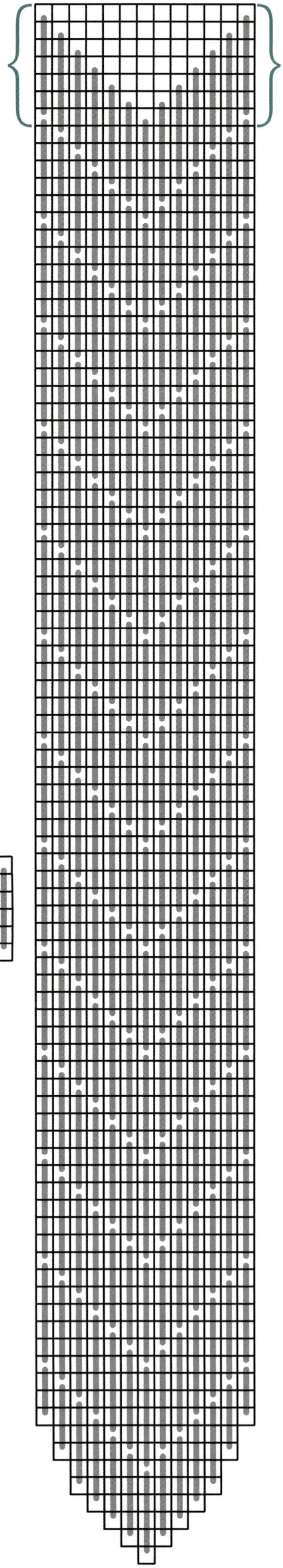

Plastic Canvas Basics

WORKING WITH PLASTIC CANVAS

Counting Threads. The lines of the canvas are referred to as threads. They are not actually "threads" since the canvas is not woven. Before cutting out your pieces, note the thread count of each chart which is listed near the chart. It indicates the number of threads in the width and height of the canvas piece. To cut pieces accurately, count **threads** (not **holes**) as shown in **Fig. 1**.

Fig. 1

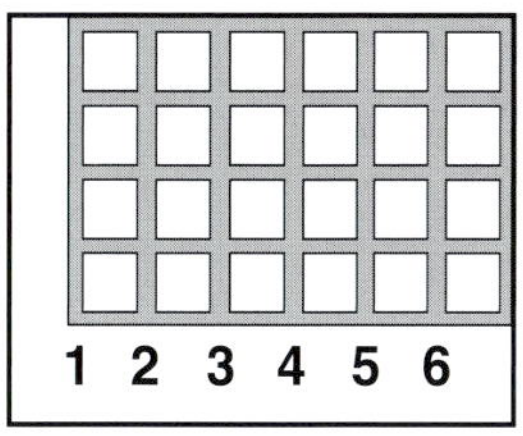

Marking the Canvas. You may want to mark the outline of the piece on your canvas before cutting it out. Use a China marker or a grease pencil to draw the outline on the canvas. Cut out the shape and remove all markings with a dry paper towel.

Cutting the Canvas. Cut as close to the thread as possible without cutting into the thread. "Nubs" left on the edge of your canvas will snag the yarn and are difficult to cover. A craft knife is helpful when cutting a small area from the center of a piece of canvas. Alaways cut on a layer of cardboard or a magazine.

WORKING WITH YARN

Selecting Yarn. We used various brands of worsted weight/medium weight yarn to stitch the photography models for this book. It is important to buy all of the yarn you need to complete your project from the same dye lot.

READING THE KEY

Color keys are included for each project. The key indicates the color of yarn used and how each color is represented on the chart. For example, when blue yarn is represented by a green line in the color key, all green stitches on the chart should be stitched using blue yarn. Yarn yardage amounts are also included on the color keys.

READING THE CHART

Whenever possible, the drawing on the chart looks like the completed stitch. To determine how a particular stitch is worked, refer to the Stitch Diagrams.

STITCHING THE DESIGN

Securing the First Stitch. Begin each yarn length by coming up from the wrong side of the canvas and leaving a 1"-2" tail on the wrong side. Hold this tail against the canvas and work the first few stitches over the tail. When secure, clip the tail close to the stitched piece.

Using Even Tension. Keep your stitching tension consistent, with each stitch lying flat and even on the canvas.

Ending Your Stitches. After you've completed all of the stitches of one color in an area, end your stitching by running the needle under several stitches on the back of the stitched piece; trim the excess yarn.

JOINING PIECES

Straight edges. The most common method of assembly is to join canvas pieces along a straight edge using overcast stitches. Place one piece on top of the other. Make sure the edges being joined are even, then stitch the pieces together through all layers.

Uneven edges. Sometimes you'll have to join diagonal edges. The holes of the two pieces will not line up exactly. Just keep the pieces even and work overcast stitches through the holes as many times as necessary to completely cover the canvas.

Shaded areas. Don't work stitches in a colored shaded area until the project instructions say you should.

STITCH DIAGRAMS

*Unless otherwise indicated, bring the threaded needle up at **1** and all **odd** numbers and down **2** and all **even** numbers.*

TENT STITCH

This stitch is worked in horizontal or vertical rows over one intersection as shown in Fig 2. Refer to Fig. 3 to work the reversed tent stitch.

Fig. 2

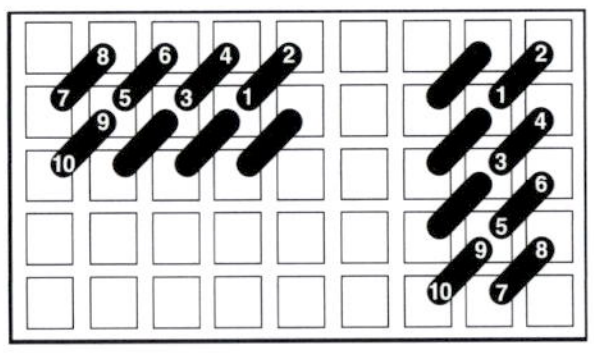

Fig. 3

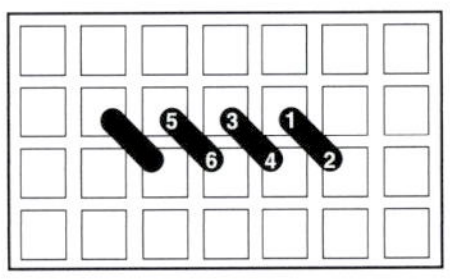

GOBELIN STITCH

This basic straight stitch is worked over two or more threads or intersections *(Fig. 4)*. The number of threads or intersections may vary according to the chart.

Fig. 4

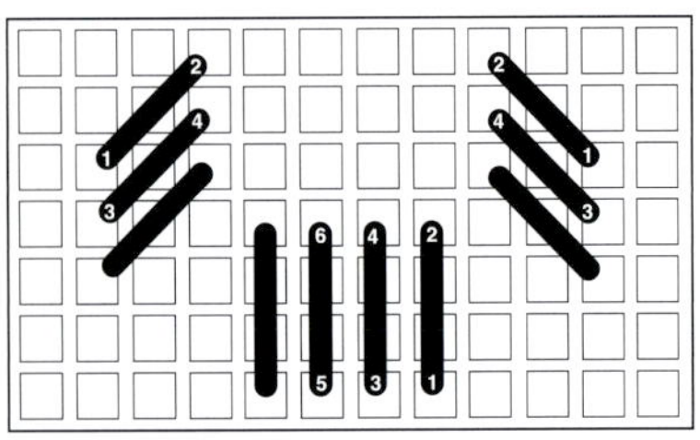

CROSS STITCH

This stitch is composed of two stitches *(Fig. 5)*. The top stitch of each cross must always be made in the same direction.

Fig. 5

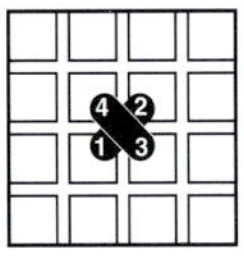

DOUBLE CROSS STITCH

This star-shaped stitch can be worked over any even number of threads *(Fig. 6)*.

Fig. 6

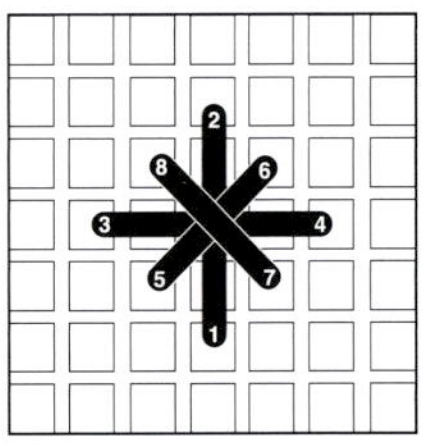

OVERCAST STITCH

This stitch covers the edge of the canvas *(Fig. 7)* and is used to join canvas pieces. It may be necessary to go through the same hole more than once to get even coverage on the edge, especially at the corners.

Fig. 7

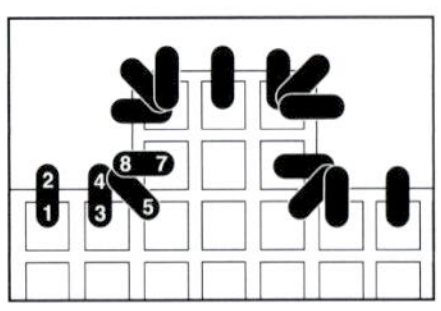

Meet Nicole Barrett

A classical pianist and young mother, Nicole Barrett has fond childhood memories of being creative with plastic canvas.

"I have been working with plastic canvas since I was a young girl spending the summers at my Oma's cottage in Northern Ontario," she says. "I wanted to make a simple crown and magic wand for my daughter's second birthday," she says. "She loved them so much, and our family and friends thought they were just wonderful, so I began to plan more designs."

Rule the Kingdom (#6916) is Nicole's first book with Leisure Arts. She also offers patterns and finished projects through Barrett Design Studio on Etsy.com.

Copyright © 2017 by Leisure Arts, Inc., 104 Champs Blvd., STE 100, Maumelle, AR 72113-6738, www.leisurearts.com. All rights reserved. This publication is protected under federal copyright laws. Reproduction or distribution of this publication or any other Leisure Arts publication, including publications which are out of print, is prohibited unless specifically authorized. This includes, but is not limited to, any form of reproduction or distribution on or through the Internet, including posting, scanning, or e-mail transmission.

We have made every effort to ensure that these instructions are accurate and complete. We cannot, however, be responsible for human error, typographical mistakes, or variations in individual work.

Production Team: Technical Writer – Jean Lewis; Technical Associates – Mary Sullivan Hutcheson and Janie Wright; Editorial Writer – Susan Frantz Wiles; Senior Graphic Artist – Lora Puls; Graphic Artist – Victoria Temple; Photostylist and Illustrator – Lori Wenger; Photographer – Jason Masters